UNLOCKING C PROGRAMMING POWER

ADVANCED PRACTITIONER TECHNIQUES

OLIVER LUCAS JR

TABLE OF CONTENTS

Chapter 1

Chapter 2

Chapter 3

Chapter 4

Chapter 5

Chapter 6

Chapter 7

Chapter 8

Chapter 9

Chapter 10

Preface

This book, "Unlocking C Programming Power: Advanced Practitioner Techniques," is not for the faint of heart. It's for those who have already tasted the power and versatility of C, who have wrestled with pointers and memory management, and who are hungry to push their skills to the next level.

If you're looking for another introductory C programming book, this isn't it. We assume you've mastered the fundamentals. Instead, we delve into the depths of C, exploring the nuances, the optimizations, and the techniques that separate experienced C programmers from the novices.

Within these pages, you'll find explorations of advanced memory management, concurrency, performance optimization, and low-level programming techniques. We dissect complex data structures, unravel the mysteries of the C preprocessor, and guide you through the intricacies of debugging and testing.

This book is a distillation of years of experience, hard-won battles with complex code, and a passion for pushing the boundaries of what's possible with C. It's a guide for those who want to write code that is not just functional, but elegant, efficient, and robust.

Whether you're building high-performance applications, delving into the world of embedded systems, or simply seeking to deepen your understanding of this powerful language, this book will be your companion on the journey.

So, buckle up, sharpen your coding tools, and prepare to unlock the true power of C programming.

Who Should Read This Book

This book is targeted at experienced C programmers who:

Have a solid understanding of C fundamentals, including pointers, memory management, and data structures.

Want to deepen their knowledge of C and explore advanced techniques.

Are interested in writing high-performance, efficient, and robust C code.

Are involved in systems programming, embedded systems development, or other areas where C excels.

How to Use This Book

This book can be read sequentially, or you can dive into specific chapters based on your interests and needs. Each chapter builds upon the previous ones, but we've also strived to make each chapter relatively self-contained.

The code examples in this book are designed to be practical and illustrative. We encourage you to experiment with the code, modify it, and adapt it to your own projects.

Acknowledgments

We would like to thank the countless C programmers and developers who have contributed to the C community and inspired us with their work. We are also grateful to the reviewers and editors who helped shape this book into its final form.

Finally, we thank you, the reader, for embarking on this journey with us. We hope this book empowers you to unlock the full potential of C programming and create amazing software.

Chapter 1

Memory Mastery

1.1 Deep Dive into Dynamic Memory Allocation

In C, we have two primary ways to manage memory: statically (at compile time) and dynamically (at runtime). While static allocation is straightforward, it has limitations. Dynamic memory allocation, on the other hand, provides the flexibility to request and release memory as needed during a program's execution. This is essential for handling data structures that grow or shrink, optimizing memory usage, and responding to unpredictable memory requirements.

The Mechanics of Dynamic Memory Allocation

At the heart of dynamic memory allocation in C lies the **heap**. This is a region of memory that the operating system sets aside for a program to use during its runtime. When you request memory using functions like `malloc`, `calloc`, or `realloc`, the system carves out a chunk of the heap and gives your program a pointer to it. This pointer acts as your handle to that memory block, allowing you to store and manipulate data within it.

Key Functions

`malloc`: This function allocates a block of memory of a specified size (in bytes). It returns a void pointer (`void *`) to the beginning of the allocated block. It's your responsibility to cast this pointer to the appropriate data type.

calloc: Similar to malloc, but it also initializes all the bytes in the allocated memory block to zero. This can be crucial for security and for simplifying the initialization of data structures.

realloc: This function allows you to resize a previously allocated memory block. It can expand or shrink the block as needed. This is essential for dynamic arrays and other data structures that change size during program execution.

free: This function is the counterpart to the allocation functions. It's absolutely critical to use free to release any dynamically allocated memory when you're finished with it. Failing to do so leads to memory leaks, which can eventually exhaust system resources and cause program instability.

Advanced Considerations

Memory Alignment: The system often allocates memory in blocks that are aligned to specific memory addresses (e.g., multiples of 4 or 8 bytes). This is important for performance reasons, especially when dealing with certain data types or hardware architectures.

Fragmentation: As you repeatedly allocate and free memory blocks, the heap can become fragmented. This means that even if there's enough total free memory, there might not be a single contiguous block large enough to satisfy a new request. Fragmentation can lead to performance degradation.

Error Handling: It's crucial to always check the return values of memory allocation functions. If they fail (e.g., if malloc returns NULL), it means the system couldn't provide the requested memory. Robust error handling is essential to prevent program crashes.

Beyond the Basics

For advanced C programmers, mastering dynamic memory allocation goes beyond simply knowing how to use `malloc` and `free`. It involves understanding the underlying mechanisms, optimizing memory usage, and employing advanced techniques like custom memory allocators and memory pools to improve performance and prevent memory-related issues.

This "deep dive" sets the stage for the rest of the chapter, where we'll explore these advanced concepts and techniques in detail, providing practical examples and insights to help you write robust and efficient C code.

1.2 Advanced Pointer Manipulation and Arithmetic

Pointers are a cornerstone of C programming, providing a powerful mechanism for direct memory access and manipulation. While fundamental pointer concepts are essential, advanced C practitioners need to go further, understanding the intricacies of pointer arithmetic and mastering techniques for complex pointer manipulation. This section delves into these advanced aspects, equipping you with the skills to wield pointers effectively in demanding scenarios.

Pointer Arithmetic: Beyond the Basics

Pointer arithmetic in C is more than just incrementing or decrementing pointers. It involves understanding how pointers interact with data types and memory addresses.

Pointer Arithmetic and Data Types: When you perform arithmetic on a pointer, the change in its address is scaled by the size of the data type it points to. For example, incrementing an integer pointer (`int *`) moves it forward by `sizeof(int)` bytes, not just 1 byte. This ensures that the pointer always points to the beginning of the next element in an array or data structure.

Pointer Arithmetic and Arrays: Pointers and arrays have a close relationship in C. An array name can often be treated as a pointer to its first element. This allows you to use pointer arithmetic to traverse arrays efficiently, access elements at specific offsets, and perform operations on array elements without using array indexing.

Pointer Arithmetic and Memory Addresses: Pointers essentially hold memory addresses. Understanding how these addresses are represented and manipulated is crucial for advanced pointer usage. We'll explore how to calculate address offsets, perform pointer comparisons, and work with pointers to different data types.

Advanced Pointer Manipulation Techniques

Beyond basic arithmetic, advanced pointer manipulation involves techniques for working with complex data structures and performing intricate memory operations.

Pointers to Pointers: We'll explore the concept of pointers to pointers (e.g., `int **`), which are often used to create dynamic multi-dimensional arrays, linked lists of pointers, and other complex data structures. Understanding how to allocate, access, and manipulate these pointers is essential for advanced C programming.

Function Pointers: Function pointers allow you to store the address of a function and call it indirectly. This enables powerful techniques like dynamic function dispatch, callbacks, and creating flexible and extensible code. We'll delve into the syntax and usage of function pointers, along with their applications in various programming scenarios.

Void Pointers: Void pointers (`void *`) are generic pointers that can point to any data type. They are often used in functions that need to work with different data types or when the exact type is not known at compile time. We'll discuss how to use void pointers safely and effectively, including proper casting and type checking.

Caveats and Considerations

Memory Safety: Pointer arithmetic can be powerful, but it also comes with risks. Incorrect pointer operations can lead to memory corruption, program crashes, and security vulnerabilities. We'll emphasize the importance of careful pointer manipulation, bounds checking, and defensive programming techniques to prevent these issues.

Code Readability: Complex pointer expressions can be difficult to read and understand. We'll discuss strategies for writing clear and maintainable code when working with advanced pointer techniques, including using meaningful variable names, comments, and code structuring.

By mastering advanced pointer manipulation and arithmetic, you'll gain a deeper understanding of C's memory model and unlock powerful techniques for working with data structures, optimizing performance, and writing more sophisticated and flexible code.

1.3 Preventing and Debugging Memory Leaks

Memory leaks are a common and insidious problem in C programming, especially in applications that deal with dynamic memory allocation. They occur when allocated memory blocks are no longer needed but are not properly released back to the system using `free`. Over time, these leaks can accumulate, consuming valuable system resources and potentially leading to performance degradation, instability, and even program crashes. This section equips you with the knowledge and techniques to prevent and debug memory leaks, ensuring the robustness and efficiency of your C programs.

Prevention Strategies

Careful Memory Management: The most fundamental way to prevent memory leaks is to practice meticulous memory management. This means:

Allocate only what you need: Avoid allocating excessively large memory blocks.

Free memory when done: Always release allocated memory using `free` when it's no longer required.

Match every `malloc` **with a** `free`: Ensure a one-to-one correspondence between memory allocation and deallocation.

Structured Programming Techniques:

RAII (Resource Acquisition Is Initialization): This principle suggests tying resource management (like memory allocation) to object lifetimes. When an object goes out of scope, its destructor automatically releases the associated resources.

Clear Code Structure: Maintain a well-organized code structure to make it easier to track memory allocation and deallocation. Use functions and modules to encapsulate memory management logic.

Defensive Programming:

Error Handling: Implement robust error handling to catch potential allocation failures (`malloc` returning NULL) and handle them gracefully to prevent leaks in error scenarios.

Null Pointer Checks: Before freeing memory, ensure the pointer is not NULL to avoid program crashes.

Tools and Libraries:

Smart Pointers: Consider using smart pointers (available in C++ or through libraries like Boehm GC) to automate memory management and reduce the risk of leaks.

Static Analysis Tools: Employ static analysis tools to identify potential memory leaks and other code issues during development.

Debugging Techniques

Memory Debuggers:

Valgrind: This powerful tool can detect memory leaks, memory corruption, and other memory-related errors. It provides detailed reports to help pinpoint the source of leaks.

AddressSanitizer (ASan): Another valuable tool that can detect memory errors like use-after-free, buffer overflows, and memory leaks.

Manual Debugging:

Logging and Tracing: Add logging statements to track memory allocation and deallocation events. This can help you identify areas of your code where leaks are likely to occur.

Code Reviews: Have other developers review your code to identify potential memory management issues.

Best Practices

Document Memory Management: Clearly document your memory allocation and deallocation strategies in your code and documentation.

Test Thoroughly: Test your code rigorously, including stress testing and long-running tests, to uncover memory leaks that might not be apparent during normal usage.

Stay Informed: Keep up-to-date with the latest memory management techniques and tools to improve your skills and prevent memory-related problems.

By combining preventive measures with effective debugging techniques, you can minimize the risk of memory leaks and ensure that your C programs are robust, efficient, and reliable.

Chapter 2

Performance Optimization

2.1 Profiling and Benchmarking C Code

Performance optimization is a critical skill for advanced C programmers. To write truly efficient code, you need to identify bottlenecks, measure execution times, and understand how your code interacts with the system's resources. This section explores two essential techniques for achieving this: profiling and benchmarking.

Profiling: Unveiling Performance Hotspots

Profiling is the process of analyzing a program's execution to identify which parts of the code consume the most time or resources. This helps you pinpoint performance bottlenecks and focus your optimization efforts where they will have the greatest impact.

Types of Profiling:

CPU Profiling: Measures the time spent in different functions or code sections.

Memory Profiling: Tracks memory usage, identifies memory leaks, and helps optimize memory allocation patterns.

I/O Profiling: Analyzes input/output operations, which can be a significant source of performance overhead.

Profiling Tools:

gprof: A traditional profiling tool that provides function-level timing information.

perf: A powerful performance analysis tool available on Linux systems, offering a wide range of profiling capabilities.

Valgrind (Callgrind): Can be used for detailed call graph analysis and performance profiling.

Analyzing Profiling Data:

Identify Hotspots: Pinpoint the functions or code sections that consume the most CPU time or memory.

Understand Call Graphs: Visualize the relationships between functions and identify potential areas for optimization.

Focus Optimization Efforts: Use the profiling data to guide your optimization strategies and prioritize the most impactful changes.

Benchmarking: Measuring Performance

Benchmarking involves systematically measuring the performance of your code under controlled conditions. This allows you to compare different implementations, evaluate the impact of optimizations, and track performance improvements over time.

Benchmarking Methodology:

Establish a Baseline: Measure the performance of your initial code version to establish a baseline for comparison.

Isolate Code Sections: Focus on benchmarking specific code sections or functions to get accurate measurements.

Control the Environment: Ensure consistent testing conditions by controlling factors like system load, compiler settings, and input data.

Repeat Measurements: Run benchmarks multiple times to account for variations and obtain statistically significant results.

Benchmarking Tools and Techniques:

Timers: Use high-resolution timers like `clock_gettime` to measure execution times accurately.

Performance Counters: Access hardware performance counters to gather detailed information about CPU cycles, cache misses, and other performance metrics.

Benchmarking Frameworks: Consider using benchmarking frameworks (like Google Benchmark) to streamline the benchmarking process and generate meaningful reports.

Combining Profiling and Benchmarking

Profiling and benchmarking are complementary techniques. Profiling helps you identify *where* to optimize, while benchmarking helps you measure *how much* your optimizations improve performance. By combining these approaches, you can gain a deep understanding of your code's behavior and achieve significant performance gains.

Key Considerations:

Overhead: Be aware that profiling can introduce some overhead, which might slightly affect performance measurements.

Accuracy: Strive for accurate and reliable benchmarking results by controlling variables and repeating measurements.

Relevance: Choose benchmarking scenarios that are relevant to your application's real-world usage patterns.

By mastering profiling and benchmarking techniques, you can transform your C code from functional to highly efficient, ensuring that it performs optimally in demanding environments.

2.2 Algorithmic Efficiency and Optimization Strategies

In the realm of C programming, crafting efficient algorithms is paramount, especially when dealing with complex tasks and large datasets. This section dives into the core principles of algorithmic efficiency and explores various optimization strategies that can significantly enhance the performance of your C code.

Understanding Algorithmic Efficiency

Before diving into optimization, it's crucial to grasp the concept of algorithmic efficiency. This refers to how effectively an algorithm utilizes computational resources, primarily time and memory.

Time Complexity: This measures how the running time of an algorithm grows with the size of the input data. It's commonly expressed using Big O notation (e.g., $O(n)$, $O(n \log n)$, $O(n^2)$), which provides an upper bound on the growth rate.

Space Complexity: This measures how much memory an algorithm uses as the input size increases. It's also expressed using Big O notation, indicating the growth rate of memory usage.

Analyzing the time and space complexity of your algorithms is essential for understanding their scalability and identifying potential bottlenecks.

Optimization Strategies

Once you have a good understanding of your algorithm's efficiency, you can apply various optimization strategies to improve its performance.

Choose the Right Data Structures: Selecting appropriate data structures can drastically impact performance. For example, using a hash table for frequent lookups can be much faster than using an array or linked list.

Reduce Algorithm Complexity: Strive to design algorithms with lower time complexity. For instance, if you have a nested loop with $O(n^2)$ complexity, try to find an alternative approach with $O(n \log n)$ or $O(n)$ complexity.

Loop Optimization:

Loop Unrolling: Reduce loop overhead by repeating the loop body multiple times within a single iteration.

Loop Fusion: Combine multiple loops that iterate over the same data into a single loop.

Reduce Function Calls: Function calls have overhead. Minimize unnecessary function calls by inlining small functions or using macros (with caution).

Bitwise Operations: Utilize bitwise operations for faster arithmetic and logical operations, especially when dealing with flags or low-level data manipulation.

Memory Optimization:

Minimize Memory Allocation: Reduce the number of dynamic memory allocations by reusing memory or using stack-allocated variables when possible.

Improve Data Locality: Accessing data in a contiguous manner improves cache utilization and reduces memory access times.

Compiler Optimizations: Utilize compiler optimization flags (e.g., -O2, -O3) to enable the compiler to perform various optimizations, such as code inlining, loop unrolling, and dead code elimination.

Advanced Techniques

Dynamic Programming: Break down complex problems into smaller overlapping subproblems and store their solutions to avoid redundant computations.

Greedy Algorithms: Make locally optimal choices at each step to find a global optimum. This is effective for certain optimization problems.

Divide and Conquer: Recursively break down a problem into smaller subproblems, solve them independently, and combine their solutions.

Profiling and Benchmarking

Use profiling tools (like gprof or perf) to identify performance bottlenecks in your code. Benchmark your code to measure the impact of optimizations and compare different implementations.

Key Considerations:

Readability: While optimization is crucial, don't sacrifice code readability. Strive for a balance between performance and maintainability.

Trade-offs: Be aware of potential trade-offs between time and space complexity. Some optimizations might improve speed but increase memory usage.

Testing: Thoroughly test your code after applying optimizations to ensure correctness and avoid introducing new bugs.

By understanding algorithmic efficiency and applying effective optimization strategies, you can write C code that performs at its best, handling complex tasks with speed and efficiency.

2.3 Bitwise Operations and Low-Level Optimization

C provides a set of bitwise operators that allow you to manipulate data at the bit level. While these operators might seem arcane at first, they offer powerful capabilities for low-level optimization, especially when dealing with tasks that require precise control over individual bits or when performance is paramount.

Bitwise Operators: A Quick Refresher

AND (&): Sets each bit to 1 if both corresponding bits are 1.

OR (|): Sets each bit to 1 if at least one of the corresponding bits is 1.

XOR (^): Sets each bit to 1 if only one of the corresponding bits is 1.

NOT (~): Inverts all the bits.

Left Shift (<<): Shifts the bits to the left by a specified number of positions.

Right Shift (>>): Shifts the bits to the right by a specified number of positions.

Low-Level Optimization Techniques

1 Bit Manipulation:

Setting and Clearing Bits: Use bitwise AND, OR, and NOT to efficiently set, clear, or toggle individual bits within a data value. This is often used for managing flags, status registers, or bitmasks.

Extracting Bits: Use bitwise AND and right shift to extract specific bits or bit fields from a value.

2 Arithmetic Operations:

Multiplication and Division by Powers of 2: Left and right shift operations can be significantly faster than traditional multiplication and division when working with powers of 2.

Modulo Operations: For certain modulo operations (e.g., modulo 2), bitwise AND can be more efficient than the modulo operator (%).

3 Data Packing and Unpacking:

Storing Multiple Values in a Single Variable: Use bitwise operations to pack multiple small values into a single variable, reducing memory usage and improving data locality.

Efficient Data Serialization: Bitwise operations can be used to efficiently serialize and deserialize data for storage or transmission.

4 Low-Level System Programming:

Hardware Interaction: Bitwise operations are essential for interacting with hardware devices, setting registers, and controlling device behavior at the bit level.

Memory Management: Bitwise operations can be used for tasks like memory alignment and addressing.

Examples

Setting a Bit:

C

```
unsigned char flags = 0; // Initial flags
```

```c
flags |= (1 << 3);          // Set the 4th bit
(0-indexed)
```

Checking if a Bit is Set:

C

```c
if (flags & (1 << 3)) {

    // The 4th bit is set

}
```

Fast Multiplication by 4:

C

```c
int x = 10;

int result = x << 2; // Equivalent to x * 4
```

Caveats and Considerations

Code Readability: Bitwise operations can make code less readable, especially for those unfamiliar with them. Use comments and meaningful variable names to improve clarity.

Portability: Be mindful of potential portability issues when using bitwise operations, especially when dealing with signed integers and right shifts.

Compiler Optimizations: Modern compilers are often capable of optimizing basic arithmetic operations into bitwise equivalents. However, understanding bitwise operations allows you to perform more advanced optimizations and fine-tune your code for specific scenarios.

By mastering bitwise operations, you gain a deeper understanding of how data is represented and manipulated at the hardware level. This knowledge enables you to write highly optimized C code, especially for performance-critical applications and low-level system programming tasks.

Chapter 3

Concurrency and Parallelism

3.1 Threads, Processes, and Synchronization Primitives

When writing advanced C programs, you'll often need to go beyond the sequential execution model and leverage the power of concurrency. This involves understanding the concepts of threads, processes, and the synchronization primitives that allow them to cooperate and share resources safely.

Processes

A process is an independent running program with its own memory space, resources, and execution context. Think of it as a self-contained unit of work.

Characteristics:

Isolation: Processes have their own memory space, protecting them from interfering with each other.

Resource Ownership: Each process has its own set of resources (memory, file descriptors, etc.).

Heavier Weight: Creating and managing processes can be relatively resource-intensive.

Threads

A thread is a lightweight unit of execution within a process. Multiple threads can exist within the same process, sharing the same memory space and resources.

Characteristics:

Shared Memory: Threads within a process share the same memory space, allowing for efficient communication and data sharing.

Lightweight: Creating and switching between threads is generally faster than working with processes.

Concurrency: Threads can execute concurrently, potentially utilizing multiple CPU cores for parallel processing.

Synchronization Primitives

When multiple threads access shared resources concurrently, there's a risk of race conditions and data corruption. Synchronization primitives provide mechanisms to control access to shared resources and ensure thread safety.

Mutexes (Mutual Exclusion):

Purpose: A mutex is like a lock that only one thread can acquire at a time. This ensures exclusive access to a shared resource, preventing race conditions.

Usage: Threads acquire the mutex before accessing the shared resource and release it when done. Other threads trying to acquire the mutex will block until it's released.

Semaphores:

Purpose: A semaphore is a counter that can be used to control access to a limited number of resources.

Usage: Threads "wait" on a semaphore to acquire a resource. If the semaphore count is greater than zero, the thread decrements the count and proceeds. If the count is zero, the thread blocks until a resource becomes available. When a thread is done with a resource, it "signals" the semaphore, incrementing the count.

Condition Variables:

Purpose: A condition variable allows threads to wait for a specific condition to become true.

Usage: Threads can "wait" on a condition variable, blocking until another thread "signals" that the condition has been met. This is often used to synchronize threads based on events or state changes.

Example (Mutex)

C

```c
#include <pthread.h>



pthread_mutex_t mutex; // Declare a mutex



// ...



pthread_mutex_lock(&mutex); // Acquire the mutex

// Access the shared resource

pthread_mutex_unlock(&mutex);    // Release the
mutex
```

Choosing the Right Primitive

The choice of synchronization primitive depends on the specific needs of your program.

Mutexes: Ideal for protecting single shared resources.

Semaphores: Useful for managing a pool of resources or implementing producer-consumer patterns.

Condition Variables: Suitable for synchronizing threads based on events or conditions.

Important Considerations

Deadlocks: Avoid situations where two or more threads are blocked indefinitely, waiting for each other to release resources.

Performance: Excessive synchronization can lead to performance bottlenecks. Strive for a balance between thread safety and efficiency.

Complexity: Concurrent programming can be complex. Carefully design and test your code to avoid race conditions and other concurrency issues.

By mastering threads, processes, and synchronization primitives, you can write powerful C programs that leverage concurrency for improved performance and responsiveness.

3.2 Inter-Process Communication (IPC) Techniques

In complex C applications, you often need to go beyond the confines of a single process and enable communication and data exchange between different processes. This is where Inter-Process Communication (IPC) techniques come into play. IPC mechanisms provide ways for processes to cooperate, share data, and synchronize their actions, enabling you to build sophisticated distributed systems and applications.

Why IPC?

Modularity: Break down large applications into smaller, independent processes that can communicate with each other.

Parallelism: Utilize multiple processes to perform tasks concurrently, potentially leveraging multiple CPU cores for improved performance.

Specialization: Create specialized processes for specific tasks, improving efficiency and resource utilization.

Fault Tolerance: Isolate processes to prevent errors in one process from affecting others.

Common IPC Techniques

1 Pipes:

Mechanism: A pipe is a unidirectional communication channel that connects two related processes. One process writes data to the pipe, and the other reads from it.

Types:

Anonymous Pipes: Used for communication between parent and child processes.

Named Pipes (FIFOs): Can be used for communication between unrelated processes on the same system.

2 Message Queues:

Mechanism: A message queue is a kernel-maintained data structure that allows processes to send and receive messages asynchronously.

Features:

Asynchronous Communication: Processes can send messages without waiting for the receiver to be ready.

Message Types: Messages can have different types, allowing for more structured communication.

3 Shared Memory:

Mechanism: Processes share a region of memory that they can both read from and write to.

Features:

Fast Communication: Shared memory provides the fastest form of IPC because processes access data directly in memory without kernel intervention.

Synchronization: Requires careful synchronization to prevent race conditions and data corruption.

4 Sockets:

Mechanism: Sockets provide a network-based communication mechanism, allowing processes on the same or different machines to communicate.

Features:

Network Communication: Enables communication over various network protocols (TCP/IP, UDP).

Versatility: Can be used for both local (inter-process) and remote (client-server) communication.

5 Signals:

Mechanism: Signals are software interrupts that can be sent to a process to notify it of an event.

Usage:

Event Notification: Signals can be used to notify a process of events like a timer expiration, a child process termination, or an error condition.

Interruption: Signals can interrupt a process's normal execution flow.

Choosing the Right Technique

The choice of IPC technique depends on factors like:

Performance: Shared memory is generally the fastest, followed by pipes and message queues. Sockets can have higher overhead due to network communication.

Complexity: Pipes are relatively simple to use, while shared memory requires careful synchronization.

Communication Pattern: Consider whether you need one-way or two-way communication, synchronous or asynchronous communication.

Distance: For communication between processes on different machines, sockets are the primary choice.

Example (Pipe)

C

```c
#include <unistd.h>
```

```c
int fd[2];

pipe(fd); // Create a pipe


if (fork() == 0) { // Child process

    close(fd[1]); // Close the write end

    // Read from fd[0]

} else { // Parent process

    close(fd[0]); // Close the read end

    // Write to fd[1]

}
```

By mastering IPC techniques, you can build powerful and flexible C applications that leverage the full capabilities of modern operating systems and distributed environments.

3.3 Designing Concurrent Data Structures

When venturing into the world of concurrent programming in C, you'll inevitably encounter the challenge of designing data structures that can be safely and efficiently accessed by multiple threads simultaneously. This is where the art of designing concurrent data structures comes into play. It requires careful consideration of synchronization, data consistency, and performance to create robust and scalable solutions.

Challenges in Concurrent Data Structures

Race Conditions: Multiple threads accessing and modifying a shared data structure concurrently can lead to race conditions, where the final outcome depends on the unpredictable timing of thread execution.

Data Corruption: Without proper synchronization, concurrent access can corrupt the internal state of a data structure, leading to unpredictable behavior and program crashes.

Deadlocks: Threads can become deadlocked if they are waiting for each other to release locks on shared resources, resulting in a program freeze.

Performance Bottlenecks: Excessive synchronization can hinder performance by creating contention and limiting parallelism.

Approaches to Designing Concurrent Data Structures

1 Fine-Grained Locking:

Mechanism: Use multiple locks to protect specific parts of the data structure.

Benefits: Allows for higher concurrency as different threads can access different parts of the data structure simultaneously.

Challenges: Requires careful lock management to avoid deadlocks and ensure correctness.

2 Lock-Free Data Structures:

Mechanism: Employ atomic operations and careful memory management to avoid the use of locks altogether.

Benefits: Can achieve higher performance and scalability by eliminating lock contention.

Challenges: Significantly more complex to design and implement correctly. Requires a deep understanding of memory models and concurrency primitives.

3 Optimistic Concurrency Control:

Mechanism: Threads operate on a copy of the data structure and attempt to merge their changes back to the original. Conflicts are detected and resolved if necessary.

Benefits: Can improve performance in scenarios with low contention.

Challenges: Requires efficient conflict detection and resolution mechanisms.

4 Concurrent Collections:

Mechanism: Use pre-built concurrent data structures provided by libraries or frameworks.

Benefits: Simplifies development and reduces the risk of errors.

Examples: The C++ standard library provides concurrent data structures like `std::atomic`, `std::mutex`, and concurrent queues.

Design Considerations

Synchronization: Choose appropriate synchronization primitives (mutexes, semaphores, condition variables) to ensure thread safety and prevent race conditions.

Granularity of Locking: Balance the granularity of locking to maximize concurrency while minimizing overhead.

Data Consistency: Maintain data consistency by ensuring that operations on the data structure are atomic and that invariants are preserved.

Performance: Optimize for performance by minimizing lock contention, reducing overhead, and maximizing parallelism.

Complexity: Strive for simplicity and clarity in your design to reduce the risk of errors and improve maintainability.

Examples

Concurrent Queue: A queue that can be safely accessed by multiple threads for enqueue and dequeue operations.

Concurrent Hash Table: A hash table that allows concurrent insertions, deletions, and lookups.

Thread-Safe Linked List: A linked list that can be safely traversed and modified by multiple threads.

Tools and Techniques

Formal Verification: Use formal methods to verify the correctness of your concurrent data structure design.

Stress Testing: Test your data structure under high concurrency to identify potential race conditions or performance bottlenecks.

Code Reviews: Have other developers review your code to identify potential concurrency issues.

Designing concurrent data structures is a challenging but essential skill for advanced C programmers. By carefully considering synchronization, data consistency, and performance, you can create robust and scalable solutions that enable efficient concurrent programming.

Chapter 4

Advanced Data Structures

4.1 Hash Tables and Efficient Hashing Algorithms

Hash tables are powerful data structures that provide efficient key-value storage and retrieval. They achieve this by using a hash function to map keys to indices in an array (the hash table). This allows for near-constant-time average complexity for insertion, deletion, and lookup operations, making hash tables a valuable tool in many applications.

How Hash Tables Work

1 Hash Function: A hash function takes a key as input and produces an integer (the hash code) as output. This hash code is then used to determine the index in the hash table where the corresponding value will be stored.

2 Hash Table (Array): The hash table itself is an array of "buckets" or "slots." Each bucket can hold one or more key-value pairs.

3 Collision Handling: When two different keys hash to the same index (a collision), a collision resolution strategy is needed. Common strategies include:

Separate Chaining: Each bucket holds a linked list or another data structure to store multiple key-value pairs that hash to the same index.

Open Addressing: If a collision occurs, the algorithm probes other locations in the hash table according to a predefined rule (linear probing, quadratic probing, double hashing) until an empty slot is found.

Efficient Hashing Algorithms

The choice of hash function is crucial for the performance of a hash table. A good hash function should:

Be Fast to Compute: Hashing should be a quick operation to avoid adding significant overhead.

Distribute Keys Evenly: The hash function should distribute keys uniformly across the hash table to minimize collisions.

Minimize Collisions: Even with a good distribution, collisions are inevitable. The hash function should aim to minimize the number of collisions.

Common Hashing Algorithms

Modular Hashing: A simple and common approach where the hash code is calculated as the remainder of the key divided by the table size.

C

```c
int hash(int key, int table_size) {

    return key % table_size;

}
```

Multiplicative Hashing: Multiplies the key by a constant and takes the fractional part of the result. This helps to distribute keys more evenly.

Bitwise Operations: For integer keys, bitwise operations (XOR, shifting) can be used to create efficient hash functions.

Cryptographic Hash Functions: For security-sensitive applications, cryptographic hash functions (like SHA-256) provide strong collision resistance but can be computationally more expensive.

Advanced Hashing Techniques

Perfect Hashing: For a fixed set of keys, perfect hashing can guarantee no collisions. This is often used in applications like compilers and interpreters.

Consistent Hashing: Distributes keys across a cluster of servers in a way that minimizes data movement when servers are added or removed.

Universal Hashing: Uses a family of hash functions, randomly selecting one at runtime to provide better average-case performance against adversarial input.

Optimizing Hash Tables

Load Factor: The load factor is the ratio of the number of elements to the table size. A high load factor can increase collisions and degrade performance. Consider resizing the hash table when the load factor exceeds a certain threshold.

Table Size: Choose a table size that is a prime number to improve key distribution and reduce collisions.

Collision Resolution: Select a collision resolution strategy that balances performance and memory usage. Separate chaining is often preferred for its simplicity and good performance.

Applications of Hash Tables

Associative Arrays: Hash tables are commonly used to implement associative arrays or dictionaries, providing efficient key-value storage and retrieval.

Databases: Hash tables are used for indexing in databases to speed up data access.

Caches: Caches often use hash tables to store frequently accessed data for quick retrieval.

Compilers: Compilers use hash tables for symbol table management.

By understanding hash tables and efficient hashing algorithms, you can leverage their power to optimize data storage and retrieval in your C programs. Choosing the right hash function and collision resolution strategy is crucial for achieving optimal performance and scalability.

4.2 Trees: Binary Search Trees, AVL Trees, and Tries

Trees are fundamental data structures in computer science, resembling hierarchical structures with a root node and branches leading to child nodes. They are versatile and efficient for organizing and managing data, and this section explores three important types of trees: Binary Search Trees, AVL Trees, and Tries.

Binary Search Trees (BSTs)

A Binary Search Tree is a binary tree with a special property: for each node, all the values in its left subtree are smaller than its value, and all the values in its right subtree are greater. This property enables efficient searching, insertion, and deletion operations.

Operations:

Insertion: Start at the root and traverse down the tree, comparing the new value with the current node's value. Insert the new node as a leaf when an appropriate position is found.

Deletion: Deleting a node can be more complex, depending on whether the node has zero, one, or two children. Special cases need to be handled to maintain the BST property.

Search: Start at the root and traverse down the tree, comparing the target value with the current node's value. Go left if the target is smaller, right if it's larger.

Time Complexity:

Best Case (Balanced Tree): O(log n) for search, insertion, and deletion.

Worst Case (Skewed Tree): O(n) for search, insertion, and deletion.

AVL Trees

AVL trees are self-balancing binary search trees. They maintain a balance factor (the difference in height between the left and right subtrees) of at most 1 for each node. This ensures that the tree remains relatively balanced, preventing worst-case scenarios and guaranteeing logarithmic time complexity for most operations.

Balancing: AVL trees use rotations (single and double rotations) to rebalance the tree when insertions or deletions cause an imbalance.

Time Complexity:

O(log n) for search, insertion, and deletion in all cases.

Tries (Prefix Trees)

Tries are specialized tree-like structures used for efficient prefix searching. They are often used for storing and searching strings or sequences of characters.

Structure: Each node in a trie represents a character, and paths from the root to nodes represent prefixes of strings.

Operations:

Insertion: Traverse the trie based on the characters in the string, creating new nodes as needed.

Search: Traverse the trie based on the characters in the search string.

Prefix Search: Find all strings with a given prefix.

Applications:

Autocomplete: Suggesting words or phrases as the user types.

Spell Checking: Efficiently checking the spelling of words.

IP Routing: Storing and searching network prefixes for efficient routing.

Choosing the Right Tree

BSTs: Simple to implement but can become unbalanced, leading to poor performance in the worst case.

AVL Trees: Guarantee logarithmic time complexity but are more complex to implement due to the balancing operations.

Tries: Specialized for prefix searching and efficient for string-related operations.

Example (BST in C)

```c
C

struct Node {

    int data;

    struct Node *left;

    struct Node *right;

};
```

```
//  ...  (functions  for  insertion,  deletion,
search)
```

By understanding the characteristics and trade-offs of different tree structures, you can choose the most suitable one for your specific needs and optimize your C programs for efficient data management and retrieval.

4.3 Graphs and Graph Algorithms

Graphs and graph algorithms are a fascinating and essential area of computer science. Here's a breakdown to get us started:

Graphs: A Foundation

A graph is a fundamental data structure that represents relationships between objects. It consists of:

Vertices (Nodes): The objects or entities in the graph.

Edges: The connections or relationships between vertices.

Graphs can be:

Directed: Edges have a direction (e.g., a one-way street).

Undirected: Edges have no direction (e.g., a friendship connection).

Weighted: Edges have associated weights (e.g., the distance between two cities).

Unweighted: Edges have no weights.

Graph Representations

Adjacency Matrix: A 2D array where `matrix[i][j]` indicates an edge between vertex `i` and `j`.

Adjacency List: An array of lists where each list stores the neighbors of a vertex.

Essential Graph Algorithms

Graph algorithms are used to solve various problems on graphs, such as:

Traversal:

Breadth-First Search (BFS): Explores the graph level by level.

Depth-First Search (DFS): Explores the graph by going as deep as possible along each branch before backtracking.

Shortest Path:

Dijkstra's Algorithm: Finds the shortest paths from a single source vertex to all other vertices in a weighted graph with non-negative edge weights.

Bellman-Ford Algorithm: Finds the shortest paths from a single source vertex to all other vertices in a weighted graph, even with negative edge weights (but no negative cycles).

Floyd-Warshall Algorithm: Finds the shortest paths between all pairs of vertices in a weighted graph.

Minimum Spanning Tree (MST):

Prim's Algorithm: Finds a minimum spanning tree for a weighted, connected, undirected graph.

Kruskal's Algorithm: Another algorithm for finding a minimum spanning tree.

Other Algorithms:

Topological Sort: Orders the vertices of a directed acyclic graph (DAG) such that for every directed edge (u, v), vertex u comes before vertex v in the ordering.

Strongly Connected Components: Finds groups of vertices in a directed graph where every vertex is reachable from every other vertex within the same group.

Applications of Graph Algorithms

Social Networks: Analyzing connections between people.

Maps and Navigation: Finding shortest routes and directions.

Network Routing: Optimizing data flow in computer networks.

Recommendation Systems: Recommending products or content based on relationships between users and items.

Data Mining: Discovering patterns and relationships in large datasets.

Chapter 5

Working with the File System

5.1 File I/O Operations and System Calls

File I/O (Input/Output) operations are fundamental to many C programs, allowing them to interact with the file system to read, write, and manipulate files. These operations are typically performed through system calls, which are requests made to the operating system's kernel.

System Calls: The Bridge to the Kernel

System calls provide a controlled interface for user programs to access and utilize operating system services, including file I/O. When a program makes a system call, it temporarily transfers control to the kernel, which executes the requested operation and returns the result to the program.

Key File I/O System Calls

`open()`:

Purpose: Opens a file and returns a file descriptor, an integer that represents the file within the program.

Parameters:

`pathname`: The path to the file.

`flags`: Flags specifying how the file should be opened (e.g., read-only, write-only, create if it doesn't exist, append).

`mode`: (Optional) Permissions to set if the file is created.

`close():`

Purpose: Closes a file descriptor, releasing the associated resources.

Parameter: The file descriptor to close.

`read():`

Purpose: Reads data from a file.

Parameters:

`fd`: The file descriptor.

`buf`: A buffer to store the read data.

`count`: The maximum number of bytes to read.

`write():`

Purpose: Writes data to a file.

Parameters:

`fd`: The file descriptor.

`buf`: A buffer containing the data to write.

`count`: The number of bytes to write.

`lseek()`:

Purpose: Changes the file offset (the current position for reading or writing).

Parameters:

`fd`: The file descriptor.

`offset`: The offset to move to.

`whence`: Specifies the starting point for the offset (e.g., beginning of the file, current position, end of the file).

Example (Reading from a File)

C

```c
#include <fcntl.h>

#include <unistd.h>

#include <stdio.h>


int main() {

    int fd = open("myfile.txt", O_RDONLY);

    if (fd == -1) {

        perror("open");

        return 1;

    }
```

```c
    char buffer[1024];

        ssize_t  bytes_read  =  read(fd,  buffer,
sizeof(buffer));

    if (bytes_read == -1) {

        perror("read");

        close(fd);

        return 1;

    }



    printf("Read %zd bytes: %s\n", bytes_read,
buffer);


    close(fd);

    return 0;

}
```

Error Handling

It's crucial to check the return values of system calls for errors. Most file I/O system calls return -1 on error and set the `errno` variable to indicate the specific error that occurred. The `perror()` function can be used to print an error message based on `errno`.

File I/O in C Standard Library

The C standard library (`stdio.h`) provides a higher-level interface for file I/O, built on top of the system calls. Functions like `fopen()`, `fclose()`, `fread()`, `fwrite()`, and `fseek()` offer a more convenient way to work with files.

Advanced File I/O

File Locking: Use `fcntl()` to lock files or parts of files to prevent concurrent access and ensure data integrity.

Asynchronous I/O: Use functions like `aio_read()` and `aio_write()` to perform I/O operations asynchronously, allowing the program to continue execution while I/O is in progress.

Memory Mapping: Use `mmap()` to map a file directly into memory, allowing you to access the file's contents as if it were an array in memory.

By understanding file I/O operations and system calls, you gain direct control over how your C programs interact with the file system. This knowledge is essential for developing applications that handle files efficiently and reliably.

5.2 Directory Traversal and Manipulation

In C programming, interacting with the file system often involves more than just reading and writing files. You might need to navigate through directories, create new directories, or delete existing ones. This is where directory traversal and manipulation techniques come in. These techniques allow you to programmatically explore and modify the directory structure, enabling you to build applications that manage files and directories efficiently.

System Calls for Directory Operations

Several system calls provide the foundation for directory traversal and manipulation in C:

`opendir():`

Purpose: Opens a directory and returns a directory stream, a pointer to a `DIR` structure that represents the directory.

Parameter: The path to the directory.

`readdir():`

Purpose: Reads the next directory entry from a directory stream.

Parameter: The directory stream.

Returns: A pointer to a `dirent` structure containing information about the directory entry (file name, type, etc.), or NULL if there are no more entries or an error occurs.

`closedir():`

Purpose: Closes a directory stream, releasing the associated resources.

Parameter: The directory stream.

```
mkdir():
```

Purpose: Creates a new directory.

Parameters:

`pathname`: The path to the new directory.

`mode`: Permissions to set for the new directory.

```
rmdir():
```

Purpose: Removes an empty directory.

Parameter: The path to the directory.

```
chdir():
```

Purpose: Changes the current working directory.

Parameter: The path to the new working directory.

Example (Listing Directory Contents)

C

```c
#include <stdio.h>

#include <dirent.h>


int main() {
```

```c
    DIR *dir = opendir("."); // Open the current
directory

    if (dir == NULL) {

        perror("opendir");

        return 1;

    }


    struct dirent *entry;

    while ((entry = readdir(dir)) != NULL) {

        printf("%s\n", entry->d_name);

    }


    closedir(dir);

    return 0;

}
```

Traversing Directory Hierarchies

To traverse directory hierarchies (explore subdirectories), you can combine the `opendir()` and `readdir()` functions with recursion. When you encounter a directory entry that is itself a directory, you can recursively call the traversal function on that subdirectory.

Manipulating Directories

Creating Directories: Use `mkdir()` to create new directories. You can create multiple levels of directories by specifying the full path in the `pathname` parameter.

Removing Directories: Use `rmdir()` to remove empty directories. To remove directories that contain files or subdirectories, you'll need to first delete their contents recursively.

Renaming and Moving: Use the `rename()` system call to rename files or directories. This can also be used to move a file or directory to a different location.

Error Handling

As with file I/O, it's essential to check the return values of directory-related system calls for errors. Most of these calls return -1 or NULL on error and set the `errno` variable to indicate the specific error.

Advanced Techniques

Glob Patterns: Use the `glob()` function to find files that match a specific pattern (e.g., `*.txt`).

Symbolic Links: Create symbolic links (shortcuts) to files or directories using the `symlink()` system call.

File Permissions: Use the `chmod()` system call to change the permissions of files and directories.

By mastering directory traversal and manipulation techniques, you can write C programs that interact with the file system in sophisticated ways, organizing and managing files and directories efficiently.

5.3 Efficient File Processing Techniques

When working with files in C, especially large files or those that require frequent access, efficiency becomes paramount. This section explores various techniques and strategies to optimize file processing operations, minimizing overhead and maximizing performance.

1. Buffering

Concept: Instead of reading or writing data one byte or character at a time, buffering involves reading or writing larger chunks of data into a buffer (a temporary storage area in memory). This reduces the number of system calls and disk accesses, significantly improving performance.

Types:

Fully Buffered: Data is transferred to/from the buffer only when it's full or explicitly flushed.

Line Buffered: Data is transferred when a newline character is encountered.

Unbuffered: Data is transferred immediately without buffering.

Implementation:

Standard I/O Library: The `stdio.h` library provides buffered I/O through functions like `fread()` and `fwrite()`. You can adjust the buffer size using `setvbuf()`.

Manual Buffering: For more control, you can implement your own buffering mechanism using arrays or dynamically allocated memory.

2. Block I/O

Concept: Read and write data in blocks (chunks) that align with the file system's block size. This optimizes data transfer and reduces the number of disk seeks.

Implementation:

`read()` **and** `write()` **System Calls:** Use these system calls directly to perform block I/O.

`posix_memalign()`: Allocate memory aligned to the file system's block size.

3. Asynchronous I/O

Concept: Perform I/O operations asynchronously, allowing your program to continue execution while the I/O operation is in progress. This can improve responsiveness and overall performance, especially when dealing with multiple files or network operations.

Implementation:

`aio_read()` **and** `aio_write()`: POSIX asynchronous I/O functions.

Callbacks: Use callbacks to be notified when an asynchronous I/O operation completes.

4. Memory Mapping

Concept: Map a file directly into your program's memory space using the `mmap()` system call. This allows you to access the file's contents as if it were an array in memory, potentially improving performance by reducing data copying and allowing the operating system to manage file caching more efficiently.

Benefits:

Efficient Access: Direct memory access to the file's contents.

Shared Memory: Can be used for inter-process communication.

Considerations:

Memory Usage: The entire file (or a portion of it) is loaded into memory.

Synchronization: If multiple processes access the mapped memory, synchronization is needed.

5. Data Structures and Algorithms

Efficient Data Structures: Choose appropriate data structures for storing and processing the data read from files. For example, hash tables can be efficient for indexing and searching.

Algorithm Optimization: Optimize the algorithms used to process the file data. For example, use sorting algorithms with good time complexity if sorting is required.

6. File Format Optimization

Compression: If applicable, use file compression techniques to reduce file size and improve I/O performance.

Binary Formats: Consider using binary file formats instead of text formats for more compact and efficient data storage.

Data Serialization: Use efficient data serialization techniques (like Protocol Buffers or Apache Avro) to store complex data structures in files.

7. System Considerations

File System Type: Different file systems have different performance characteristics. Choose a file system that is optimized for your application's needs.

Disk I/O Optimization: Consider using solid-state drives (SSDs) for faster I/O performance.

Operating System Settings: Tune operating system settings related to file caching and I/O scheduling to improve performance.

By combining these techniques and considering the specific requirements of your application, you can significantly improve the efficiency of file processing operations in your C programs.

Chapter 6

Network Programming with Sockets

6.1 Socket Programming Fundamentals (TCP/IP and UDP)

Sockets are the fundamental building blocks of network programming. They provide an interface for processes to communicate with each other, either on the same machine or across a network. This communication is facilitated by the underlying network protocols, primarily TCP/IP and UDP.

What is a Socket?

Think of a socket as an endpoint for communication. It's like a phone number that uniquely identifies a process on a network. When a process wants to communicate with another process, it creates a socket and binds it to a specific address and port number.

Key Concepts

IP Address: A unique numerical identifier for a device on a network.

Port Number: A numerical identifier that distinguishes between different applications or services running on the same machine.

TCP (Transmission Control Protocol):

Connection-oriented, reliable protocol.

Provides guaranteed delivery of data in order.

Used for applications like web browsing (HTTP), file transfer (FTP), and email (SMTP).

UDP (User Datagram Protocol):

Connectionless, unreliable protocol.

Does not guarantee delivery or order of data.

More efficient than TCP, but less reliable.

Used for applications like streaming media, DNS lookups, and online gaming.

Socket API

The socket API provides a set of functions for working with sockets. These functions are typically available in the sys/socket.h header file.

socket(): Creates a new socket.

bind(): Binds a socket to a specific address and port.

listen(): (TCP server) Listens for incoming connections on a socket.

accept(): (TCP server) Accepts a connection from a client.

connect(): (TCP client) Establishes a connection to a server.

send() / recv(): Send and receive data over a socket.

sendto() / recvfrom(): Send and receive data over a UDP socket.

close(): Closes a socket.

TCP Socket Programming

Server:

Create a socket.

Bind the socket to an address and port.

Listen for incoming connections.

Accept a connection from a client.

Send and receive data.

Close the connection.

Client:

Create a socket.

Connect to the server's address and port.

Send and receive data.

Close the connection.

UDP Socket Programming

Sender:

Create a socket.

Bind the socket (optional).

Send data to the receiver's address and port using `sendto()`.

Receiver:

Create a socket.

Bind the socket to an address and port.

Receive data using `recvfrom()`.

Example (Simple TCP Client)

C

```c
#include <sys/socket.h>

#include <netinet/in.h>

#include <stdio.h>


int main() {

    int sockfd = socket(AF_INET, SOCK_STREAM, 0);

    // ... (error handling)


    struct sockaddr_in serv_addr;

    // ... (set server address and port)


            connect(sockfd,    (struct    sockaddr
*)&serv_addr, sizeof(serv_addr));

    // ... (error handling)


    send(sockfd, "Hello from client", 18, 0);

    // ... (receive data from server)


    close(sockfd);
```

```
    return 0;

}
```

Key Considerations

Error Handling: Network programming is prone to errors (network failures, connection issues). Robust error handling is crucial.

Byte Ordering: Different machines may use different byte ordering (big-endian or little-endian). Use functions like `htons()` and `ntohl()` to convert between network byte order and host byte order.

Blocking vs. Non-blocking Sockets: Sockets can be configured to be blocking (wait for an operation to complete) or non-blocking (return immediately).

Concurrency: Handle multiple clients concurrently using techniques like multithreading or asynchronous I/O.

Socket programming is a powerful tool for building networked applications in C. By understanding the fundamentals of TCP/IP and UDP, and mastering the socket API, you can create applications that communicate effectively over networks.

6.2 Building Client-Server Applications in C

Client-server applications are the backbone of many networked systems, from web browsing to online gaming. In this model, a server provides services or resources, and clients connect to the server to request those services. This section guides you through the process of building client-server applications in C using sockets.

1. Choose a Network Protocol

TCP: Reliable, connection-oriented. Suitable for applications that require guaranteed delivery and order of data (e.g., file transfer, remote login).

UDP: Efficient, connectionless. Suitable for applications where speed is more important than reliability (e.g., streaming media, DNS lookups).

2. Design the Application

Define the Service: Clearly define the service the server will provide and the types of requests clients can make.

Data Exchange Format: Decide on a format for exchanging data between client and server (e.g., plain text, JSON, XML, a custom binary format).

Error Handling: Plan for potential errors (network failures, invalid requests) and design appropriate error handling mechanisms.

3. Implement the Server

Create a Socket: Use the `socket()` function to create a socket with the appropriate protocol (TCP or UDP).

Bind the Socket: Use the `bind()` function to bind the socket to a specific address and port number. The port number identifies the service on the server.

Listen for Connections (TCP): If using TCP, use the `listen()` function to put the socket in listening mode, ready to accept incoming connections.

Accept Connections (TCP): Use the `accept()` function to accept a connection from a client. This creates a new socket for communication with the client.

Receive and Process Requests: Use `recv()` (TCP) or `recvfrom()` (UDP) to receive data from the client. Process the request and generate a response.

Send Responses: Use `send()` (TCP) or `sendto()` (UDP) to send the response back to the client.

Close Connections (TCP): Close the connection using `close()` when communication is finished.

4. Implement the Client

Create a Socket: Use the `socket()` function to create a socket with the appropriate protocol.

Connect to the Server (TCP): If using TCP, use the `connect()` function to establish a connection to the server's address and port.

Send Requests: Use `send()` (TCP) or `sendto()` (UDP) to send requests to the server.

Receive Responses: Use `recv()` (TCP) or `recvfrom()` (UDP) to receive responses from the server.

Close the Connection (TCP): Close the connection using `close()` when finished.

5. Error Handling and Robustness

Check Return Values: Always check the return values of socket functions for errors.

Handle Network Errors: Implement strategies to handle network errors gracefully (e.g., timeouts, connection resets).

Validate Input: Validate data received from clients to prevent security vulnerabilities and ensure proper application behavior.

Example (Simple TCP Echo Server)

C

```c
// Server
#include <sys/socket.h>
#include <netinet/in.h>
#include <stdio.h>
#include <string.h>

int main() {
    // ... (create socket, bind, listen)

    while (1) {
        // ... (accept connection)

        char buffer[1024];
        int valread = read(new_socket, buffer, 1024);
        printf("Client: %s\n", buffer);
        send(new_socket, buffer, strlen(buffer), 0);

        // ... (close connection)
    }
```

```
    return 0;

}
```

Key Considerations

Concurrency: Handle multiple clients concurrently using techniques like multithreading or asynchronous I/O.

Security: Implement security measures to protect against unauthorized access and data breaches.

Performance: Optimize for performance by minimizing data transfer, using efficient data structures, and managing resources effectively.

Building client-server applications in C requires a solid understanding of socket programming and network protocols. By following these steps and considering the key factors, you can create robust and efficient networked applications.

6.3 Secure Network Communication

Security is paramount in today's interconnected world, and network communication is no exception. When building networked applications in C, especially those handling sensitive data, it's crucial to implement measures that protect against unauthorized access, data breaches, and other security threats. This section explores key concepts and techniques for securing network communication in your C programs.

1. Encryption

Purpose: Encryption transforms data into an unreadable format, preventing unauthorized parties from understanding the information even if they intercept it.

Algorithms:

Symmetric Encryption: Uses the same key for encryption and decryption. Examples: AES, DES.

Asymmetric Encryption: Uses a pair of keys (public and private). Data encrypted with the public key can only be decrypted with the private key. Examples: RSA, ECC.

Implementation:

TLS/SSL: Use libraries like OpenSSL to implement TLS/SSL (Transport Layer Security/Secure Sockets Layer), a widely used protocol for secure network communication. TLS/SSL provides encryption, authentication, and data integrity.

Custom Encryption: For specific needs, you can implement your own encryption algorithms, but be mindful of security best practices and potential vulnerabilities.

2. Authentication

Purpose: Verifies the identity of the communicating parties to ensure that they are who they claim to be.

Methods:

Passwords: Require users to provide passwords for authentication.

Digital Certificates: Use digital certificates issued by trusted authorities to verify the identity of servers or clients.

Biometrics: Use biometric data (fingerprint, facial recognition) for authentication.

Implementation:

TLS/SSL: TLS/SSL supports certificate-based authentication.

Challenge-Response: Implement challenge-response protocols where one party sends a challenge, and the other party must provide a correct response based on a shared secret.

3. Data Integrity

Purpose: Ensures that data has not been tampered with during transmission.

Methods:

Hashing: Use hash functions (like SHA-256) to generate a unique fingerprint of the data. Compare the hash of the received data with the hash of the original data to detect modifications.

Message Authentication Codes (MACs): Similar to hashing, but uses a secret key to generate the MAC, providing stronger security.

Implementation:

TLS/SSL: TLS/SSL includes mechanisms for data integrity checks.

Custom Implementations: You can implement your own data integrity checks using hashing or MAC algorithms.

4. Secure Design Principles

Principle of Least Privilege: Grant only the necessary permissions to users and processes.

Defense in Depth: Implement multiple layers of security (encryption, authentication, firewalls).

Input Validation: Validate all input from external sources to prevent injection attacks and other vulnerabilities.

Secure Coding Practices: Follow secure coding guidelines to avoid common security pitfalls (buffer overflows, format string vulnerabilities).

5. Tools and Libraries

OpenSSL: A widely used library for TLS/SSL and cryptographic operations.

Libsodium: A modern, easy-to-use library for encryption, decryption, signatures, password hashing, and more.

Network Security Tools: Use tools like Wireshark and tcpdump to analyze network traffic and identify potential security issues.

Example (TLS/SSL with OpenSSL)

```c
C

// ... (include OpenSSL headers)


SSL_CTX *ctx = SSL_CTX_new(TLS_method());

// ... (load certificates)


SSL *ssl = SSL_new(ctx);

// ... (associate SSL with socket)


SSL_connect(ssl);

// ... (secure communication)
```

```
SSL_free(ssl);

SSL_CTX_free(ctx);
```

Securing network communication is an ongoing process that requires careful consideration of potential threats and the implementation of appropriate security measures. By incorporating encryption, authentication, data integrity checks, and secure design principles, you can build C applications that communicate securely over networks.

Chapter 7

Debugging and Testing

7.1 Advanced Debugging Techniques with GDB

While GDB (the GNU Debugger) is widely used for basic debugging tasks like setting breakpoints and inspecting variables, it offers a wealth of advanced features that can significantly enhance your debugging workflow. This section explores some of these techniques, empowering you to tackle complex debugging challenges in your C programs.

1. Conditional Breakpoints

Concept: Trigger breakpoints only when a specific condition is met. This is useful for narrowing down the search for bugs that occur under specific circumstances.

Implementation:

Code snippet

```
break <location> if <condition>
```

Example: `break myfunction if x > 100`

2. Watchpoints

Concept: Monitor a variable or memory location and trigger a breakpoint when its value changes. This helps track down unexpected modifications that might be causing issues.

Implementation:

Code snippet

```
watch <expression>
```

Example: `watch myvariable`

3. Breakpoint Commands

Concept: Execute a series of GDB commands automatically when a breakpoint is hit. This can be used to print values, inspect variables, or even modify program state without manually entering commands each time.

Implementation:

Code snippet

```
commands <breakpoint number>

<command 1>

<command 2>

...

end
```

Example:

Code snippet

```
commands 1
```

```
print x

print y

continue

end
```

4. Reverse Debugging

Concept: Step backward through the execution history of your program. This allows you to understand how a particular state was reached or analyze the sequence of events leading to a crash.

Implementation:

Code snippet

```
record

// ... run your program ...

reverse-step

reverse-continue
```

5. Debugging Multi-threaded Programs

Concept: GDB provides features for debugging programs with multiple threads.

Commands:

`info threads`: List all threads.

`thread <thread number>`: Switch to a specific thread.

`break <location> thread <thread number>`: Set a breakpoint on a specific thread.

`set scheduler-locking on`: Prevent other threads from running while debugging a specific thread.

6. Examining Core Dumps

Concept: Analyze core dump files, which contain a snapshot of the program's memory at the time of a crash. This can provide valuable insights into the cause of the crash.

Implementation:

Code snippet

```
gdb <program> <core dump file>
```

7. Customizing GDB with Python

Concept: Extend GDB's functionality by writing Python scripts. This allows you to automate complex debugging tasks, create custom commands, and integrate with other tools.

Implementation:

Use the `python` command within GDB to execute Python code.

Define Python functions that can be called as GDB commands.

8. Advanced Memory Inspection

Concept: Examine memory contents in various formats and interpret data structures.

Commands:

`x/<format> <address>`: Examine memory at a specific address.

`dump memory <file> <start address> <end address>`: Dump memory contents to a file.

`find <value>`: Search for a specific value in memory.

Example (Examining Memory)

Code snippet

```
x/10i $pc    // Examine 10 instructions at the
program counter

x/4xw 0x12345678    // Examine 4 words (32-bit
values)  in  hexadecimal  format  at  address
0x12345678
```

By mastering these advanced debugging techniques with GDB, you can significantly improve your ability to diagnose and resolve complex issues in your C programs, leading to more robust and reliable software.

7.2 Unit Testing and Test-Driven Development

Unit testing and test-driven development (TDD) are essential practices for writing high-quality, reliable C code. They help you catch bugs early in the development process, improve code design, and ensure that your code behaves as expected.

Unit Testing

Unit testing involves testing individual units of code (typically functions or modules) in isolation to verify that they work correctly. Each unit test focuses on a specific aspect of the unit's behavior, providing clear and concise feedback on whether the code meets its requirements.

Benefits of Unit Testing

Early Bug Detection: Catch bugs early in the development cycle, making them easier and cheaper to fix.

Improved Code Design: Writing testable code often leads to better design choices, promoting modularity and loose coupling.

Regression Prevention: Unit tests act as a safety net, preventing regressions (reintroducing old bugs) when making changes to the code.

Documentation: Unit tests serve as a form of documentation, demonstrating how the code is intended to be used.

Confidence: A comprehensive suite of unit tests gives you confidence that your code works as expected.

Test-Driven Development (TDD)

TDD takes unit testing a step further by making it an integral part of the development process. In TDD, you follow a cycle:

1 Write a Failing Test: Before writing any code, write a unit test that defines a specific behavior or requirement. This test should initially fail because the code to implement that behavior doesn't exist yet.

2 Write the Code: Write just enough code to make the failing test pass.

3 Refactor: Improve the code's structure and readability while ensuring that all tests still pass.

Benefits of TDD

Focus on Requirements: TDD forces you to think about the desired behavior before writing the code, leading to a clearer understanding of the requirements.

Higher Test Coverage: TDD encourages you to write tests for all aspects of the code, resulting in higher test coverage and greater confidence in the code's correctness.

Better Design: TDD often leads to more modular and testable code, as you are constantly thinking about how to write code that is easy to test.

Unit Testing Frameworks in C

Several unit testing frameworks are available for C, providing tools and utilities to streamline the testing process:

Unity: A simple and popular unit testing framework for C.

CUnit: Another widely used framework with a more traditional approach.

Google Test: A comprehensive testing framework originally developed for C++ but also usable with C.

Check: A unit testing framework for C with a focus on test coverage.

Example (Unity)

```c
C

#include "unity.h"

#include "mycode.h" // Code to be tested


void test_myfunction(void) {
```

```
    TEST_ASSERT_EQUAL(42, myfunction(20, 22));

    // ... more assertions ...

}


int main(void) {

    UNITY_BEGIN();

    RUN_TEST(test_myfunction);

    // ... run more tests ...

    return UNITY_END();

}
```

Key Considerations

Test Granularity: Focus on testing small, isolated units of code.

Test Coverage: Aim for high test coverage, but prioritize critical and complex parts of the code.

Test Data: Use a variety of test data, including edge cases and invalid inputs, to thoroughly test the code's behavior.

Continuous Integration: Integrate unit testing into your continuous integration (CI) pipeline to ensure that tests are run automatically whenever code changes are made.

By embracing unit testing and TDD, you can significantly improve the quality and reliability of your C code. These practices promote good design, help you catch bugs early, and give you greater confidence in your software.

7.3 Static and Dynamic Code Analysis

Code analysis is a crucial aspect of software development, helping to identify potential issues, improve code quality, and ensure reliability. It can be broadly categorized into two main approaches: static analysis and dynamic analysis.

Static Code Analysis

Static code analysis examines the source code without actually executing it. It's like a thorough inspection of the code's structure, syntax, and semantics to identify potential problems before they manifest during runtime.

Techniques:

Lexical Analysis: Examines the code's vocabulary (keywords, identifiers, operators) for basic errors.

Syntax Analysis: Checks if the code conforms to the language's grammar rules.

Semantic Analysis: Analyzes the meaning and relationships within the code to identify potential logical errors.

Control Flow Analysis: Examines the program's execution paths to detect issues like unreachable code or infinite loops.

Data Flow Analysis: Tracks how data is used and modified throughout the program to identify potential data inconsistencies or errors.

Benefits:

Early Detection: Identifies potential issues early in the development cycle, before they become more costly to fix.

Wide Scope: Can analyze the entire codebase, even unexecuted parts.

Code Quality: Helps enforce coding standards and best practices.

Security: Can detect potential security vulnerabilities (e.g., buffer overflows, SQL injection).

Tools:

Linters: Tools like `cppcheck` and `clang-tidy` for C/C++.

Static Analyzers: More comprehensive tools like Coverity and SonarQube.

Dynamic Code Analysis

Dynamic code analysis involves running the code and observing its behavior during execution. It focuses on identifying runtime issues and performance bottlenecks.

Techniques:

Instrumentation: Adding code to track execution flow, variable values, and resource usage.

Profiling: Measuring the time spent in different parts of the code to identify performance hotspots.

Memory Analysis: Detecting memory leaks and memory corruption.

Performance Testing: Evaluating the code's performance under different load conditions.

Benefits:

Runtime Issues: Identifies issues that only manifest during execution (e.g., memory leaks, race conditions).

Performance Optimization: Pinpoints performance bottlenecks and areas for improvement.

Test Coverage: Helps assess the effectiveness of testing by identifying untested code paths.

Tools:

Debuggers: Tools like GDB and LLDB.

Profilers: Tools like `gprof` and `perf`.

Memory Debuggers: Tools like Valgrind.

Combining Static and Dynamic Analysis

Static and dynamic code analysis are complementary techniques. Static analysis catches potential issues early on, while dynamic analysis identifies runtime problems and performance bottlenecks. Using both approaches provides a more comprehensive view of the code's quality and reliability.

Key Considerations

False Positives: Static analysis tools might report false positives (issues that are not actual bugs).

Code Complexity: Dynamic analysis can be more challenging for complex codebases.

Overhead: Instrumentation for dynamic analysis can introduce some runtime overhead.

By incorporating both static and dynamic code analysis into your development process, you can significantly improve the quality, security, and performance of your C code.

Chapter 8

Metaprogramming with Macros

8.1 Preprocessor Directives and Macro Expansion

The C preprocessor is a powerful tool that manipulates your code before it reaches the compiler. It uses directives (commands that start with #) to perform various actions, including file inclusion, macro expansion, and conditional compilation. This section focuses on preprocessor directives related to macro expansion, which allows you to create symbolic names for code fragments and values, making your code more concise, readable, and maintainable.

#define Directive

The #define directive is the cornerstone of macro definition. It creates a macro, which is an association between an identifier (the macro name) and a replacement text (the macro body).

Types of Macros

1 Object-like Macros:

These macros simply replace the macro name with the specified value or text.

Example:

C

```
#define PI 3.14159
```

```
#define MAX_SIZE 100
```

2 Function-like Macros:

These macros take arguments, similar to functions. The arguments are substituted into the macro body during expansion.

Example:

C

```
#define SQUARE(x) ((x) * (x))

#define MIN(a, b) ((a) < (b) ? (a) : (b))
```

Macro Expansion

When the preprocessor encounters a macro name in the code, it replaces it with the corresponding macro body. This process is called macro expansion.

Example:

C

```
#define PI 3.14159
```

```
float  area  =  PI  *  radius  *  radius;  //  PI  is
replaced with 3.14159
```

Benefits of Macros

Code Readability: Macros can make code more readable by replacing cryptic values or complex expressions with meaningful names.

Code Maintainability: Changes to constants or expressions can be made in a single place (the macro definition) rather than throughout the code.

Code Reusability: Macros can encapsulate commonly used code fragments, promoting code reuse.

Code Optimization: In some cases, macros can be used for performance optimization by avoiding function call overhead.

Predefined Macros

The C preprocessor provides several predefined macros that give you information about the compilation environment:

`__LINE__`: The current line number in the source file.

`__FILE__`: The name of the current source file.

`__DATE__`: The date of compilation.

`__TIME__`: The time of compilation.

Advanced Macro Techniques

Stringizing Operator (#): Converts a macro argument into a string literal.

Token Pasting Operator (##): Concatenates two tokens together.

Variadic Macros: Macros that can accept a variable number of arguments (introduced in C99).

Caveats and Considerations

Side Effects: Macros can have unexpected side effects if not used carefully, especially with function-like macros that modify their arguments.

Debugging: Debugging macro-heavy code can be challenging because the debugger works with the preprocessed code.

Code Bloat: Overuse of macros can lead to code bloat (increased code size) due to repeated expansion of macro bodies.

Example (Stringizing Operator)

C

```c
#define  PRINT_VAR(var)  printf(#var  "  =  %d\n",
var)



int x = 10;

PRINT_VAR(x); // Expands to printf("x" " = %d\n",
x);
```

By understanding preprocessor directives and macro expansion, you can leverage the power of the C preprocessor to write more efficient, readable, and maintainable code. However, it's important to be mindful of the potential pitfalls and use macros judiciously.

8.2 Conditional Compilation and Code Generation

Conditional compilation is a powerful technique that allows you to control which parts of your C code are compiled based on conditions evaluated during the preprocessing stage. This enables you to create different versions of your program from a single source code, tailoring it to specific platforms, configurations, or features. It's also closely related to code generation, where you can use the preprocessor to generate code dynamically.

Directives for Conditional Compilation

`#ifdef` **and** `#ifndef`:

`#ifdef MACRO`: Checks if a macro is defined. If it is, the code block following the directive is compiled.

`#ifndef MACRO`: Checks if a macro is not defined. If it's not, the code block is compiled.

`#if`, `#elif`, **and** `#else`:

`#if expression`: Checks if an expression evaluates to true (non-zero).

`#elif expression`: Provides an alternative condition if the preceding `#if` or `#elif` condition is false.

`#else`: Specifies a code block to be compiled if none of the preceding conditions are true.

```
#endif:
```

Marks the end of a conditional compilation block.

Example

C

```c
#define DEBUG 1


int main() {

    #ifdef DEBUG

        printf("Debug mode enabled\n");

    #endif


    // ... rest of the code ...
}
```

Applications of Conditional Compilation

Platform-Specific Code: Compile different code sections for different operating systems or architectures.

C

```c
#ifdef _WIN32

    // Windows-specific code
```

```
#elif __linux__

    // Linux-specific code

#endif
```

Debugging: Include debugging code that is only compiled when a DEBUG macro is defined.

Feature Toggles: Enable or disable features at compile time.

Code Optimization: Compile different code versions based on optimization levels.

Code Generation with the Preprocessor

The preprocessor can be used to generate code dynamically by combining macros with conditional compilation. This can be useful for repetitive code patterns or creating variations of functions or data structures.

Example

C

```
#define CREATE_FUNCTION(name, type) \

    type name(type x, type y) { \

        return x + y; \

    }
```

```
CREATE_FUNCTION(add_int, int);

CREATE_FUNCTION(add_float, float);
```

Benefits

Reduced Code Duplication: Avoid writing the same code multiple times.

Improved Maintainability: Changes to the generated code can be made in a single place (the macro).

Increased Flexibility: Generate different code variations based on compile-time conditions.

Caveats

Code Readability: Complex conditional compilation and code generation can make the code harder to read and understand.

Debugging: Debugging generated code can be challenging.

Conditional compilation and code generation are powerful tools in the C preprocessor's arsenal. They allow you to write flexible and adaptable code that can be tailored to different needs and configurations. However, it's important to use these techniques judiciously to maintain code readability and avoid unnecessary complexity.

8.3 Advanced Macro Techniques and Pitfalls

While macros offer powerful capabilities for code manipulation, they also come with potential pitfalls that can lead to unexpected behavior or difficult-to-debug issues. This section delves into advanced macro techniques and highlights common pitfalls to watch out for when working with macros in C.

Advanced Techniques

1 Stringizing Operator (#)

The # operator converts a macro argument into a string literal. This is useful for generating code that involves string representations of identifiers.

Example:

C

```
#define PRINT_VAR(var) printf(#var " = %d\n", var)

int x = 10;

PRINT_VAR(x); // Expands to: printf("x" " = %d\n", x);
```

2 Token Pasting Operator (##)

The ## operator concatenates two tokens together. This is useful for creating identifiers or constructing more complex expressions dynamically.

Example:

C

```
#define CONCAT(a, b) a ## b

int CONCAT(var, 1) = 5; // Expands to: int var1 =
5;
```

3 Variadic Macros

Variadic macros (introduced in C99) can accept a variable number of arguments. This is useful for creating more flexible and generic macros.

Example:

C

```
#define LOG(...) printf(__VA_ARGS__)

LOG("This is a log message\n");

LOG("Value of x: %d\n", x);
```

3 Predefined Macros

Utilize predefined macros like __LINE__, __FILE__, __DATE__, and __TIME__ to incorporate information about the compilation environment into your code.

Example:

C

```c
#define  LOG_ERROR(msg)  printf("[%s:%d]  Error:
%s\n",  __FILE__,  __LINE__,  msg)
```

Pitfalls

1 Unexpected Side Effects

Macro arguments are expanded directly into the macro body, which can lead to unexpected behavior if the arguments have side effects (e.g., incrementing a variable).

Example:

C

```c
#define SQUARE(x)  x * x

int i = 5;

int  result  =  SQUARE(i++);  //  i  might  be
incremented multiple times!
```

2 Operator Precedence Issues

Macros don't respect operator precedence like regular C code. Use parentheses liberally to ensure correct evaluation order.

Example:

C

```
#define ADD(x, y) x + y * 2

int result = ADD(2, 3); // Might not give the
expected result
```

3 Redefinition Conflicts

Avoid redefining macros with different values, as this can lead to confusion and unexpected behavior.

4 Debugging Challenges

Debugging macro-heavy code can be difficult because the debugger works with the preprocessed code. Use `gcc -E` to view the preprocessed output and understand how macros are expanded.

4 Code Bloat

Overuse of macros can lead to code bloat (increased code size) due to repeated expansion of macro bodies.

Best Practices

Use parentheses: Enclose macro arguments and the entire macro body in parentheses to avoid operator precedence issues.

Limit side effects: Be mindful of side effects in macro arguments.

Use descriptive names: Choose meaningful names for macros to improve code readability.

Document macros: Clearly document the purpose and usage of macros.

Consider alternatives: In some cases, inline functions might be a safer and more maintainable alternative to macros.

By understanding advanced macro techniques and being aware of potential pitfalls, you can use macros effectively while minimizing the risks associated with them. Remember to use macros judiciously and prioritize code clarity and maintainability.

Chapter 9

C and System Architectures

9.1 Understanding Memory Models and Cache Locality

When writing high-performance C code, it's essential to understand how your program interacts with the computer's memory system. This involves grasping the concept of memory models and how they affect data access, as well as optimizing for cache locality to minimize memory access latencies and maximize performance.

Memory Models

A memory model defines the rules and guarantees about how memory operations (reads and writes) are ordered and observed by different threads or processors in a concurrent system. It essentially describes how memory behaves in the presence of multiple threads or processors accessing shared data.

Sequential Consistency: The simplest memory model, where all memory operations appear to happen in a single, global order. This is easy to reason about but can limit performance in multi-threaded programs.

Relaxed Memory Models: Allow for some reordering of memory operations to improve performance, as long as certain constraints are met to ensure program correctness. Examples include:

Total Store Order (TSO): Common in x86 architectures.

Partial Store Order (PSO): More relaxed than TSO.

Relaxed Memory Order (RMO): Even more relaxed, allowing for significant compiler and hardware optimizations.

Implications for C Programming:

Data Races: Understanding the memory model is crucial for avoiding data races, where multiple threads access the same memory location without proper synchronization.

Synchronization Primitives: Use appropriate synchronization primitives (mutexes, atomic operations) to ensure data consistency and prevent race conditions.

Compiler Optimizations: Be aware that compiler optimizations can reorder memory operations, potentially affecting the behavior of concurrent programs. Use compiler barriers or memory fences to enforce ordering constraints when necessary.

Cache Locality

Modern CPUs have multiple levels of cache memory (L1, L2, L3) that are much faster than main memory (RAM). Cache locality refers to the tendency of a program to access the same or nearby memory locations repeatedly. Optimizing for cache locality can significantly improve performance by reducing the number of expensive accesses to main memory.

Types of Cache Locality:

Temporal Locality: Accessing the same memory location multiple times within a short period.

Spatial Locality: Accessing nearby memory locations.

Optimizing for Cache Locality:

Data Structures: Choose data structures that promote locality. For example, arrays exhibit good spatial locality because elements are stored contiguously in memory.

Algorithm Design: Design algorithms that access data in a predictable and localized manner.

Loop Optimization: Structure loops to access data sequentially and minimize cache misses.

Memory Allocation: Allocate memory in ways that promote locality. For example, allocate related data structures close to each other in memory.

Example (Loop Optimization)

C

```c
// Poor locality: Accessing elements in a non-sequential manner

for (int i = 0; i < N; i++) {

    for (int j = 0; j < M; j++) {

        // Access element a[j][i]

    }

}



// Better locality: Accessing elements sequentially

for (int j = 0; j < M; j++) {
```

```
for (int i = 0; i < N; i++) {

    // Access element a[j][i]

}

}
```

Tools and Techniques

Profiling Tools: Use profiling tools (like `cachegrind` or `perf`) to analyze cache misses and identify areas for improvement.

Compiler Optimizations: Enable compiler optimizations that promote cache locality (e.g., loop blocking, data prefetching).

Hardware Performance Counters: Monitor hardware performance counters to measure cache hit rates and identify performance bottlenecks.

By understanding memory models and optimizing for cache locality, you can write C code that effectively utilizes the memory hierarchy and achieves high performance. This is especially important for performance-critical applications and systems programming where efficient memory access is crucial.

9.2 Compiler Optimizations and Assembly Language

Modern compilers are incredibly sophisticated tools that can transform your C code into highly optimized machine code, often surpassing the efficiency of hand-written assembly in many cases. Understanding how compilers perform these optimizations and having a basic grasp of assembly language can help you write C code that is more amenable to optimization and achieve even better performance.

Compiler Optimization Levels

Most compilers offer different optimization levels, controlled by command-line flags (e.g., -O0, -O1, -O2, -O3 for GCC). These levels represent different trade-offs between compilation time, code size, and execution speed.

-O0 **(No Optimization)**: The compiler performs minimal optimizations, focusing on fast compilation times. This is useful for debugging.

-O1 **(Basic Optimizations)**: Enables basic optimizations like dead code elimination, constant folding, and function inlining.

-O2 **(More Optimizations)**: Includes more aggressive optimizations like loop unrolling, instruction scheduling, and common subexpression elimination.

-O3 **(Aggressive Optimizations)**: Performs even more aggressive optimizations, potentially including vectorization and function cloning.

Common Compiler Optimizations

Dead Code Elimination: Removes code that is never executed.

Constant Folding: Evaluates constant expressions at compile time.

Function Inlining: Replaces function calls with the function's body, reducing function call overhead.

Loop Unrolling: Repeats the loop body multiple times to reduce loop overhead.

Instruction Scheduling: Reorders instructions to optimize for the CPU's pipeline and execution units.

Common Subexpression Elimination: Avoids redundant calculations by reusing the results of previously computed expressions.

Strength Reduction: Replaces expensive operations with cheaper equivalents (e.g., multiplication with shifts).

Vectorization: Utilizes SIMD (Single Instruction, Multiple Data) instructions to perform operations on multiple data elements simultaneously.

Assembly Language Basics

Assembly language is a low-level programming language that provides a human-readable representation of machine code. Each assembly instruction corresponds to a specific machine instruction.

Registers: CPUs have a small number of registers, which are fast memory locations used for temporary data storage and calculations.

Instructions: Assembly instructions operate on data in registers or memory. Examples include `mov` (move data), `add` (addition), `sub` (subtraction), `jmp` (jump), and `call` (function call).

Addressing Modes: Different ways to access data in memory (e.g., direct addressing, indirect addressing, indexed addressing).

Examining Assembly Output

You can use the `-S` flag with your compiler (e.g., `gcc -S mycode.c`) to generate an assembly file (`mycode.s`) that shows the assembly code produced by the compiler. Examining this output can help you understand how the compiler is optimizing your code and identify potential areas for improvement.

Writing C Code for Optimization

Use `const`: Declare variables as `const` when possible to allow the compiler to perform constant folding and other optimizations.

Avoid Global Variables: Minimize the use of global variables, as they can hinder certain optimizations.

Structure Loops Efficiently: Write loops with simple conditions and predictable access patterns to enable loop optimizations.

Use Appropriate Data Structures: Choose data structures that are efficient for the operations you need to perform.

Avoid Unnecessary Function Calls: Inline small functions or use macros (with caution) to reduce function call overhead.

Key Considerations

Compiler-Specific Optimizations: Different compilers may perform different optimizations. Refer to your compiler's documentation for details.

Optimization Trade-offs: Aggressive optimizations can sometimes increase code size or compilation time.

Profiling: Use profiling tools to identify performance bottlenecks and guide your optimization efforts.

By understanding compiler optimizations and having a basic grasp of assembly language, you can write C code that is more amenable to optimization and achieve better performance. However, remember that code readability and maintainability are also important. Strive for a balance between optimization and code clarity.

9.3 Writing Architecture-Specific Code

While C strives to be a portable language, there are times when you need to write code that is specific to a particular computer architecture. This might be to optimize performance, access specialized hardware features, or work around limitations of certain systems. This section explores the concepts and techniques involved in writing architecture-specific code in C.

1. Identifying Architecture Features

Before writing architecture-specific code, you need to identify the relevant features of the target architecture. This includes:

CPU Architecture: x86, ARM, MIPS, PowerPC, etc.

Endianness: Little-endian or big-endian.

Word Size: 32-bit or 64-bit.

Instruction Set: SSE, AVX, NEON, etc.

Memory Model: Sequential consistency, relaxed memory models.

Specialized Hardware: GPUs, FPGAs, custom accelerators.

2. Preprocessor Directives

The C preprocessor provides directives for conditional compilation, allowing you to include or exclude code based on the target architecture.

Predefined Macros: Use predefined macros to identify the architecture:

`__x86_64__` : x86-64 architecture

`__arm__` : ARM architecture

`__BYTE_ORDER__` : Byte order (`__ORDER_LITTLE_ENDIAN__` or `__ORDER_BIG_ENDIAN__`)

Custom Macros: Define your own macros for specific architecture features or configurations.

Example

C

```c
#ifdef __x86_64__

    // x86-64 specific code
```

```
#elif __arm__

    // ARM specific code

#endif
```

3. Inline Assembly

For fine-grained control, you can use inline assembly to embed assembly instructions directly into your C code. This allows you to access specialized instructions or optimize critical code sections.

Syntax:

C

```
asm (

    "assembly instructions"

    : "output operands"

    : "input operands"

    : "clobbered registers"

);
```

Example

C

```
int result;
```

```
asm ("movl %1, %%eax; addl %2, %%eax" : "=a"
(result) : "r" (a), "r" (b)); // Add two numbers
using x86 assembly
```

4. Libraries and Intrinsics

Many libraries and compiler intrinsics provide architecture-specific functions or macros that abstract away the low-level details.

SIMD Intrinsics: Use SIMD intrinsics (e.g., SSE, AVX) to perform vectorized operations.

Architecture-Specific Libraries: Utilize libraries optimized for specific architectures (e.g., BLAS for linear algebra).

5. Data Alignment and Packing

Be mindful of data alignment and packing considerations, as different architectures may have different requirements or performance characteristics.

Alignment: Ensure data structures are aligned to appropriate memory boundaries.

Packing: Control the packing of data members within structures using compiler directives (e.g., `#pragma pack`).

6. Performance Considerations

Profiling: Use profiling tools to identify performance bottlenecks and guide your architecture-specific optimizations.

Benchmarking: Compare the performance of different implementations to choose the most efficient one.

Trade-offs: Balance performance gains with code portability and maintainability.

7. Portability

When writing architecture-specific code, strive to maintain portability whenever possible.

Abstraction: Abstract away architecture-specific details behind functions or macros.

Conditional Compilation: Use conditional compilation to include or exclude architecture-specific code.

Documentation: Clearly document any architecture-specific assumptions or dependencies.

Writing architecture-specific code can be a powerful technique for optimizing performance or accessing specialized hardware features. However, it's important to be mindful of portability and maintainability. Use these techniques judiciously and strive for a balance between performance and code clarity.

Chapter 10

Beyond Standard C

10.1 Exploring C Extensions and Language Variants

While standard C provides a solid foundation for a wide range of applications, the C ecosystem extends beyond the confines of the standard. This section explores some notable C extensions and language variants that offer additional features, specialized capabilities, or alternative approaches to C programming.

1. C Extensions

C extensions are additions or modifications to the C language that provide new functionality or improve existing features. These extensions can be implemented by compilers or through external libraries.

Common C Extensions:

Inline Functions: Allow functions to be expanded inline at the call site, reducing function call overhead.

Variable-Length Arrays (VLAs): Enable arrays to have sizes determined at runtime.

Flexible Array Members: Allow structures to have a final member that is an array of unspecified size.

_Generic Keyword: Provides a way to write type-generic macros.

Attributes: Provide additional information to the compiler about variables or functions (e.g., `__attribute__((aligned))`, `__attribute__((noreturn))`).

Compiler-Specific Extensions: Compilers often provide their own extensions to the C language, offering features specific to their platforms or optimization capabilities.

2. C Language Variants

C language variants are modifications or dialects of C that introduce significant changes to the language's syntax, semantics, or features. These variants often aim to address specific needs or provide alternative programming paradigms.

Notable C Variants:

C++: An object-oriented extension of C, adding classes, inheritance, and other features.

Objective-C: Another object-oriented extension of C, used primarily for macOS and iOS development.

Cilk: A variant that extends C with support for parallel programming.

Cyclone: A safe dialect of C that aims to prevent common security vulnerabilities.

Unified Parallel C (UPC): Extends C with features for parallel programming on shared-memory systems.

3. Embedded C

Embedded C is a specialized variant of C used for programming embedded systems (microcontrollers, real-time systems). It often includes features for:

Memory Management: Direct access to memory addresses and memory-mapped peripherals.

Interrupt Handling: Responding to hardware interrupts.

Real-Time Constraints: Meeting timing deadlines and ensuring deterministic behavior.

4. Exploring New Variants

The C language continues to evolve, and new variants or extensions are occasionally proposed or developed. These might explore:

Functional Programming: Adding functional programming features to C.

Concurrency: Improving support for concurrent and parallel programming.

Safety: Enhancing type safety and memory safety.

Benefits of Exploring Extensions and Variants

Increased Functionality: Access new features or capabilities not available in standard C.

Improved Performance: Utilize architecture-specific features or optimized libraries.

Specialized Domains: Address the specific needs of embedded systems or other specialized domains.

Alternative Paradigms: Explore different programming paradigms, such as object-oriented or parallel programming.

Caveats

Portability: Extensions and variants can reduce code portability.

Compatibility: Ensure compatibility with your compiler and target platform.

Learning Curve: Learning new variants or extensions requires time and effort.

By exploring C extensions and language variants, you can expand your C programming horizons and gain access to powerful new tools and techniques. However, it's important to be mindful of portability and compatibility considerations. Choose the extensions or variants that best suit your needs and project requirements.

10.2 Integrating C with Other Languages

C, with its focus on performance and low-level access, often plays a crucial role in systems programming and performance-critical applications. However, other languages might offer higher-level abstractions, easier development, or specialized features. Integrating C with other languages allows you to leverage the strengths of both, creating powerful and versatile solutions.

Why Integrate C with Other Languages?

Performance: Utilize C for performance-critical components while using a higher-level language for other parts of the application.

Legacy Code: Integrate existing C codebases with newer applications written in other languages.

Specialized Libraries: Access libraries written in C from other languages.

Cross-Language Development: Build systems where different components are written in different languages, each chosen for its suitability to a specific task.

Common Integration Approaches

1 Foreign Function Interfaces (FFIs)

FFIs provide mechanisms for calling functions written in one language from another language. They typically involve:

Data Type Mapping: Mapping data types between the languages.

Calling Conventions: Adhering to the calling conventions of the target language (how functions are called and arguments are passed).

Name Mangling: Handling differences in how functions are named in different languages.

Examples:

Python's `ctypes`**:** Allows calling C functions from Python.

Java Native Interface (JNI): Enables Java code to call native C/C++ code.

2 Language Bindings

Language bindings are libraries or tools that provide a higher-level interface for interacting with C code from another language. They often automate tasks like data type mapping and function wrapping.

Examples:

SWIG (Simplified Wrapper and Interface Generator): Generates bindings for various languages (Python, Java, Ruby, etc.).

cppyy: Provides Python bindings for C++.

3 Shared Libraries

Compile C code into shared libraries (`.so` on Linux, `.dll` on Windows) that can be loaded and used by other languages.

4 Inter-Process Communication (IPC)

Use IPC mechanisms (pipes, sockets, message queues) for communication between processes written in different languages.

Example (Python with `ctypes`)

Python

```python
import ctypes


# Load the C library

lib = ctypes.cdll.LoadLibrary("./mylib.so")


# Call a C function

result = lib.my_c_function(10, 20)


print(result)
```

Challenges and Considerations

Memory Management: Handle memory management carefully, especially when dealing with languages that have different memory management approaches (e.g., garbage collection vs. manual memory management).

Error Handling: Implement robust error handling to catch exceptions or errors that might occur in the C code.

Data Type Compatibility: Ensure that data types are correctly mapped between the languages.

Performance Overhead: Be aware of potential performance overhead associated with language bindings or FFIs.

Choosing an Integration Approach

The choice of integration approach depends on factors like:

Languages Involved: The specific languages you are integrating.

Complexity: The complexity of the interaction between the languages.

Performance Requirements: The performance requirements of the application.

Development Effort: The amount of effort required to implement the integration.

Integrating C with other languages can be a powerful way to combine the strengths of different programming paradigms and create more versatile and efficient applications. By understanding the common integration approaches and considering the challenges involved, you can choose the best strategy for your specific needs.

10.3 The Future of C Programming

Despite being over 50 years old, C continues to be a relevant and influential programming language. Its performance, efficiency, and low-level control make it a cornerstone of systems programming, embedded systems, and performance-critical applications. But how will C adapt to the evolving landscape of technology? Here are some key trends and predictions for the future of C:

1. Continued Relevance in Core Domains

C will likely remain a dominant force in:

Operating Systems: The core of many operating systems (Linux, Windows, macOS) is written in C, and this is unlikely to change significantly.

Embedded Systems: C's efficiency and control make it ideal for resource-constrained embedded systems, including those powering the Internet of Things (IoT).

High-Performance Computing: C's performance is crucial for scientific computing, simulations, and other high-performance applications.

Databases: Many database systems rely on C for performance-critical components.

2. Evolution of the Language

The C standard continues to evolve, with new versions introducing features and improvements:

C2x: The upcoming C standard is expected to include features like improved memory safety, enhanced concurrency support, and better integration with modern hardware.

Focus on Safety and Security: Future versions of C are likely to address concerns about memory safety and security vulnerabilities, potentially through features like stricter type checking, bounds checking, and memory management enhancements.

3. Integration with Modern Technologies

C will need to adapt to integrate with modern technologies and paradigms:

Concurrency and Parallelism: Improved support for concurrent and parallel programming will be crucial for leveraging the capabilities of multi-core processors and distributed systems.

GPU Programming: Closer integration with GPUs and other accelerators will be essential for high-performance computing and machine learning applications.

WebAssembly: C's ability to compile to WebAssembly opens up opportunities for web development and client-side applications.

4. Collaboration with Other Languages

C will increasingly collaborate with other languages:

Integration: Seamless integration with languages like Python, Java, and Go will allow developers to leverage the strengths of each language.

Hybrid Systems: Systems will be built with components written in different languages, with C often handling performance-critical tasks.

5. Tooling and Ecosystem

The C ecosystem will continue to evolve:

IDEs and Debuggers: Improved IDEs and debugging tools will enhance developer productivity and code quality.

Static and Dynamic Analysis: Advanced static and dynamic analysis tools will help identify potential issues and optimize code.

Package Managers: Package managers like Conan will simplify dependency management and build processes.

Challenges and Opportunities

Memory Safety: Addressing memory safety concerns will be crucial for writing secure and reliable C code.

Concurrency: Managing concurrency effectively will be essential for leveraging modern hardware.

Talent Gap: Attracting and training new C developers will be important for the language's continued growth.

Conclusion

C's future is bright. Its performance, efficiency, and control will ensure its relevance in core domains for years to come. By adapting to new technologies, collaborating with other languages, and addressing safety and security concerns, C will remain a powerful and versatile tool for software development.